COMFORT

COMFORT

POEMS

PEGGY PERDUE

All Capps LLC

First Printing, 2023

For information about special discounts for orders of more than five copies, please contact the author at contact@peggyperdue.com.

Cover art © tmintco via Canva.com
Author photo © Allison Kwesell

ISBN 979-8-9881406-0-3

All Capps, LLC
Corvallis, Oregon
97330

For R.

And to my patrons, who have helped make this book possible:

*Mom and Dad (of course), Stephen Clay, Kimi,
Susan, Jacob, Kim, Stacey, Chris, Emilie, Paris,
Lorraine, Kevin, Cindy, and Laura*

Contents

COMFORT

On My First Dive to the Bottom of the Marina Summer before Senior Year

When I lifted John from the water,
his body didn't fight mine.
His face
had bloated and grayed. I almost
dropped him back in.
One of us, the one who would become a nurse,
caught him. I got a grip again
and we pulled him to the beach.
She tipped him on his side, swept
a finger between his teeth, pressed
the hollow of her mouth
against his. Their cheeks ballooned.
His throat
gurgled and oozed
water mixed with vomit mixed with sand.

No one told us
death looks like this.
That you can't wipe it off, how it
sticks to the skin. We were told
ashes and dust, not

drool and grit. No one told us
one day we might not think of him.
How we could forget.
No one told us a person can love you
but not know how to comfort you.
That friends one summer
might not be the next.
No one told us
a day can end with this.
That you can lose something
that never leaves you. How many days
are filled with not knowing.

Buttermilk Biscuits

Grandma's hands
were
floury. Not perfumed,
but powdery. Soft
white. The dry paleness of her
wrinkled skin working
soured dough
in her kitchen. Smells
nudging cousins from
dreams, as she spins
the turquoise bowl,
thumb and fingers flicking.
Muscle memory
I do not possess.
Her recipe
gone,
a sigh of breath on dust.

Last We Talked

Me and Matt Marley, Matt Marley and me made
what-ifs of Walt Whitman and whatchamacallthese.
We wrote writs and wagged wits and waged wars.
Today, to this day, it's too tough to think of
him. How is he, his happenings, how happy is he?
He's hung his hat or hardened his heart. He's
possibly playing the piano, pounding the porcelain
keys. Kicking. Killing? In Kabul?
Could be crying. Could be cringing. Catching me
looking. Leering into the layers of the labyrinth.
Sweetly spinning, sickeningly spiraling, swapping
revolutions. Ready to resolve what's ripping us.
Reaping what's been retched from Republicans.
Democracy's dying, and dear darlings
gnashing and gnarring, getting gnarled in the globe's great cities.
Matt Marley, Matt Marley, what do you make of me?
All these annals after, I'm asking about
you. Yearning the yearner. Yet you'll
never know I'm needlessly kneading my knuckles,
forgetting I'm forgotten, fact or fiction?
Me and Matt Marley, Matt Marley and me, made
wholes in the hollows and halves out of the holes.
Have you had your humility? How have you
been?

Crystal's Garden

The peppers you gave me are close to harvesting—
the serranos red, Big Berthas, well...big.

Onions the size of fists, carrots the kid planted
crowding each other out, the marigolds from Mom

finally blooming. The green beans stretch and swell.
I think of what you said about wishing, waiting.

How our expectations rarely meet reality.
I notice the empty space where nothing grows,

reminded of what needed nurtured. I bend down,
get on my knees, curve my hands like a trowel,

and dig, pull away soil, and make a small hole.
I drop seeds in, brush the earth back, and pat it.

A tightness in my chest works up to my throat.
I stand up, let my eyes water before walking

back to the house. It's not a long walk I have,
but when death comes, we must return to the dirt.

Endings

The day before night is hectic for home.
Blue clouds swallow pink sky. Trees become black.
We turn our grief to what must be done
and let go of the remainder.

The apple trees' growth has been sudden.
Fragrance of bruised fruit mixes with pine,
healing dry dirt. Another thud of flesh
and seed and core and meat

as we raise our glasses and toast, ache in our knuckles,
through our shoulders, and down into our lower backs.
We wait for sleep to tell us the unknown, wait
for hope in the dark in the moment just before light.

In Sorrow Thou Shalt Bring Forth Children

It weighs heavy
round, ripe,
like fruit.
Obvious before
the green around me.
Everyone looks
admiring,
lustful even.
It is a joy for them
to watch me grow,
placental tissue,
plump with life's continuance.
No one sees the miseries,
the sadness I contain.
But if I cry I will rot,
if I crack, they won't want me.

Night Shift

He didn't.
He did.
If he did, you do it.
If he did, he blew it.
I'm going to bed.
I'm going to change him.
Fine.
...Oh, he's fine.

Love in Embrace

Why Mama? I don't know
what death is. But birth

is the womb of the ocean
breathing over the lands.

Her children grew.
Butterflies in her stomach,

somersaulting to sounds of jazz
on the piano, pictures of them

white on a black screen.
For a summer, there was nothing

but preparing for what she couldn't see.
And so, with a sigh she released them.

Come back to me. I will watch for you.
You will know me by the heat of my blood.

In this singular calm, she put her palm on their backs,
and kissed their heads like a postmark.

I'm Not Relaxing While It's Sunny

The pain is

slow, nesting.
Each day starts overcast
by intense sunshine.

Spring
inspires gratitude and grief.
Distracted by the zoom of a curve.

A cancer frustrating
the lungs overwhelmed by
pomegranate seeds

wedding
to balls of snow. In fall, it returns.
I wake to a curious family—I am the new housekeeper.

Productive parenting
looks like a hectic jackrabbit,
shredder of travel plans,

rewarding
the dog with lemon bars,
making our own masala,

grounding
the kids in loving, laughter.
Tiny moments

the most enlightening:
I'm thankful
for a paperclip,

accomplishing
what I cannot:
keeping it all together.

By evening,
I drink whiskey from the moonshine,
tired already from the early worry of tomorrow.

Sweet Potato Pie

Now, I reck'n y'all don' know
th' "e" in "pie" is silent. Jus' like
the "you" in "y'uns" ain't ne'r
pronounced.

    Y'see, 'round 'ere we ain't got
no time fer sound'n fine. Blame't
'n th' heat.

    We don' cr'ss 'r tees, 'r got
ner ayes t' dot neither. When yer
'ere, ya gotta learnt' c'nserve a li'l.
Say thangs…slow.

    Don' rais'a huff, 'r yer arms
too much. 'Cept t' swatta awnry fly,
'r maybe wave yer hands a li'l to
cool y'self off. That why we got
them fans in back th' church pews.

    'Bout th'nly time we start a fuss
is on Sunday.

    That faint'ns real—'n I'll tell
y'all a secret—it ain't the Holy Ghost
always, neither. Nah. Don' y'all go
think'n we're that back'ard.

    It's hot a' hell down 'ere, 'n
we know't. 'S why Ma's laid up in

hospital. Got fever. None doctor's
know what 'is.

Mem'ry's go'n too. Got the
dementia. Won' eat nuth'n. Na'even
my cornbread dress'n.

Wast'n 'way. Can' holda spoon
e'en. Or suck througha straw.

Pray th' g'd Lahd tek'r home
in 'Is arms when 'E's ready. Jus'
the way she used t'do me 'en I
was li'l.

Nah, reck'n y'all don't know
'less ya live 'ere. Wh't the heat and
Holy Spir't can do fer ya. How it
comf'rts. Like a bre'ze 'n a hot day
jus' b'fore a lightn'n storm.

'N when yer troubled, 's like
th' cool arms of Ma wrapped
'round yer whole self like a
mem'ry.

We Are Meant to Be Here

A leg flops from the crumple of colors—
a rainbow of socks, underwear, stains, and pajamas.
If I could, I'd toss them all
to their corresponding geographies:

orange to burn in the sun,
turquoise into the ocean to be ripped by waves
(please don't let the fish feed on the polyester)
and yellow over my son's head

so he's dressed. The plates stack in the sink,
clothes wrinkle on the armchair, and the computer
plays videos from snacktime to lunch
so I can think.

How have we come to this?
Wildfires, homeless, the lack
of a lead for my article due tonight.
But my thoughts drift and I float

from the dining table, grab leftovers from the fridge.
The microwave is monotone as it beeps
its orders: one minute on high.
My son wants to watch something else.

I think to shoo him outside,
but it's cold and misty; and I don't want to
put him in more layers just to take them all off again.
I tell myself, tomorrow—tomorrow we'll go out.

The microwave says nothing when it's finished.
My son sits down to eat and I place food
in front of him. Across the table, I eat,
notebook ready. I watch my son

as he slurps spaghetti. He says something
unintelligible, but I laugh anyway.
He has sauce instead of gums framing
his not so baby white teeth.

How to Do Anything Better

This simple recipe was created for the hungry family—easy, fast, delicious. The secret? Start with what you've got:

2 cups boiling water
2 cups cold water
1 box gelatin mix
1 can assorted fruit (optional)

To put this meal together for the best presentation, and greatest chance of success, take advantage of all your senses:

1. See your daughter float into the kitchen and turn her face up to the stove.
2. Hear her ask what's for dinner.
3. Smell the toast from this morning's breakfast that she couldn't eat because you burned it.
4. Taste the saliva pool on your tongue as you try to answer.
5. Feel the space between your hip bones and ribs.

Finally, make it look effortless:

Tell her you're making Jell-O. She delights at dessert for dinner and hops down the hall to her room. She doesn't need to know there wasn't food enough for tomorrow.

Drive Through

dark night
pulled from
warm beds
sleeping
journey
south in
summer
in the
ford e-
series
to see
family
dreaming
black trees
stilly
march as
we slit
our eyes
waking
light that
demarks
our way
arriving

for a
weekend
maybe
longer

Fork

I still smell the mix of metal and sweat of the hands that buried me—
my back hot from digging my own grave—cool dirt strangles my neck—
the slow rust of time begins—I rest, undying, until my next undertaker
might find me—warm air at last the earth has moved from around me—
inside family prepare the last meal—his mother calls—Dinner!

Valedictorian Speech

Fellow students,

Today I speak to you alone.
We don't know the next time we'll be allowed to gather.

Here we are.
Separated in our homes staring at screens the world says we're
addicted to, as if we have a choice, instead of sitting shoulder to
shoulder, face to face.
Surrounded by a struggling world.

Some of us have lost grandparents, some parents, to a pandemic, and
most of us are here now without them watching, or by our side.
Many of us have forfeited tournaments and practices, but more than
that, we've missed long bus rides home learning to cope with wins,
losses, schoolwork, teachers, and who's broken up with whom.

We have rented images of prom from brothers and sisters, classes
before, and those that will come after us.
But then again, maybe there will never be prom again. Is this the New
Normal everyone speculates about?
And where do we fit in?

We are not the class of pomp and circumstance.
We are not the class of normal.
We are not the class of lightheartedness, silly nights out, or even long
summer days spent with friends.
Will we even have a summer?

No, we are not the class of pomp and circumstance.

We are the class that broke a pandemic.
We are the class that altered an election.
We are the class that washed our hands
And cleaned the sky.

We are not the class of pomp and circumstance.
We are the class that survived.
We are the class with hindsight, foresight, and renewed sight.
We are the class of 2020.

for Grace

The Story of Snow

Child,

>fleeting.

>>Dance in the swirls arms outstretched with one and another, let go.

Boy,

>drifting.

>>Chase the wind, eyes up, never arriving fast enough. Move slow.

Son,

>blinding.

>>Gaze out upon the mass of fated weightlessness, ashen glow.

Man,

>settling.

>>See, as each falls? Burying itself among its kin below.

Generations

Green leaves curling from a pale, thin seed
stretching, pulling, pushing—freed!
Like pink flesh emerging, shiver in the cold.
But these, these babies from barren soil hold
all fruits of life from couplets grow
of rain of sun to live to sow
future generations' food for soul.
Drink up, fill full your bodies whole
to combat hunger, mind's starvation.
On fattened fingers count enumeration
till mother comes and picks off leaves
to feed her babies that snot their sleeves
so they can grow to go to seed, that rots
before it meets the ground. Terra cotta pots
are broken. Somewhere on earth on edges
of concrete paths a child acknowledges
a green leaf curling from a pale, thin seed
stretching, pulling, pushing, freed.

Sky as Seen by Puddle

stand   in the tree roots water   ice
holding   brittle testimony of motion   stillness
breaks   leaves fallen terminal   buds
grow   from rings around yesterday   years
multiply   through fingered tributaries   rivers
explore   edges between hardness   acceptance

I Woke to Make Love

A day of clearing.
I don't know how long I watched him.
Has it really been a lifetime? The last ones in on
the joke. We draped our fingertips over coffee mugs. The steam
tropical and depleting. How much more could I sustain
the long warm autumn before winter?
I woke to longing, the flesh of human hope.

My Name Is

Poetry. I come from
Nowhere particular, a wide spot in a
Midwest
Gravel road.
We watched the cornfields grow,
Skated the frozen puddles.
My eyes filled with sky, and I followed.

My name is
Truth. I come from the Deep
South.
Front porch, waiting for storms to come in.
This hospitality makes me uneasy.
Everyone knows
My business, but it's none of theirs.

My name is
Change. I come from waters.
Northwest
Oceans pushing, rivers drinking,
Grounds drying.
Rains crowd, but there is no more land to
carry me.

My name is
Not important. I come from
Unknown
Straits through peril and experiences.
I can feel
the path behind me.
But I'm not going that way.

Acknowledgments

I am grateful to the editors of *Abandoned Mine*, where an earlier version of the poem "How to Do Anything Better" was first published and included in the anthology *43 Poems for People Who Don't Read Poetry* (2023).

Also, a very special thank-you to John Morrison, Michelle Delaine Williams, and David Backes for reading and giving feedback on an early draft of this manuscript. Their comments and edits saved me.

To Matthew Dickman and Amy Miller, who led workshops where some of these poems were seeded.

Finally, to the Atheneum fellows, faculty, and staff at the Attic Institute of Arts and Letters who stewarded me through one of the most difficult and important years of my career.

Special thanks: This book was made possible in part by a generous donation from Clay Perdue. Thank you.

www.ingramcontent.com/pod-product-compliance
Lightning Source LLC
Chambersburg PA
CBHW061448160726
47995CB00003B/1083